HIGH INCOME
GUIDE

AFTERSHOCK'S

HIGH INCOME GUIDE

Discover the Powerful Secrets to Achieving Superior Returns

BY ANDREW PACKER & THE FINANCIAL BRAIN TRUST
A Moneynews.com Publication

contents

.... **PART THREE** ....

*How to Get Your Retirement Income Portfolio on Track With a
Three-Step Plan to Generate Substantial Income in Your Retirement Years*

Retirement Has Become a Pipe Dream for Millions of Americans

Typically, Americans have relied on three financial sources to secure their "golden years": Social Security, retirement accounts, and the value of their homes when they sell to downsize.

This diversification provided for a safe, sturdy, and worry-free retirement, akin to the three legs a stool needs to be stable.

Unfortunately, that nest egg people counted on is no longer there: Social Security benefits are designed only to provide a minimum standard of living. Retirement savings are not as high as most had hoped due to a lost decade in stocks. Home values, typically the single largest source of wealth for middle-class America, have plunged and aren't likely to rise anytime soon.

This problem can't be fixed with a few weekends working overtime. The job market remains weak, and many are simply hoarding cash out of fear of unemployment (or the next market crash).

Many baby boomers set to retire already have deferred for a few years (if they're lucky). That's probably because they don't have the kind of nest egg they need to retire. It's shocking how little the average boomer has saved for retirement. It's nowhere near $1 million, a number that could fund a middle-class lifestyle for a 20-year retirement. It's nowhere near half that, $500,000, which, invested properly, could do almost the same.

The average boomer has saved less than one year's salary for retirement.

A recent survey by Wells Fargo revealed that the average boomer has about $29,000 saved up for retirement, down from $34,000 before the credit crisis. Most boomers will have to find a job they love, because they're not leaving the workplace *anytime* soon. Meanwhile, for those fortunate and frugal enough to build up a substantial nest egg, typical sources of retirement income such as bonds and CDs have meager yields.

In some cases, the yields on government TIPS (Treasury Inflation-Protected Securities) have been negative, meaning investors bought the bond *knowing* they'd take a loss!

How we got here is no surprise. Low yields on bonds and CDs are just part of the problem. Investors also face the challenge of ultra-low interest rates set by Federal Reserve Chairman Ben Bernanke. And that's to say *nothing* about Washington's insane out-of-control spending sending our debt to exceed $15 trillion. Now that our federal debt is so high, the U.S. has no choice but to "default" on its debts through massive inflation.

In this report, I hope to give you the tools you need to save your retirement. How? Primarily by showing you little-known income-generating investments that you can buy right now. That's because, whether you're near retirement or not, it's income that plays a driving role in your ability to retire with the lifestyle you want.

Some income-producing assets turned out to be toxic, like subprime mortgage bonds that nearly brought down the financial sector in 2008. So it's not *just* income that today's investors need, it's *safe* income.

The investments in this report are designed to help investors generate loads of cash in spite of the ultra-low interest rates currently set by the Federal Reserve. Some investments even kick out monthly dividend payments, unlike bonds. Some have exposure outside the United States, giving you diversification away from the dollar.

Adding a mix of these investments can reduce risk in your portfolio, substantially boost your income, and in some cases provide capital gains.

But before we get to that, I need you to understand the current investment horizon.

Americans aren't just being hit with poor returns in stocks and housing. There's a political angle, including the greatest secret that politicians and central bankers don't want to mention: a "stealth tax" that destroys returns.

Today's Retirees Face Significant Headwinds

CHAPTER 1

The Stealth Tax Takes the Biggest Bite of All

The biggest tax you pay isn't on your 1040 form. You won't find it listed with your property at City Hall. It doesn't show up on any of your utility bills, or on your brokerage statement.

It's a "stealth tax" quietly eating away at *all* of your wealth, not just your house. It hits your investments. It hits you at the gas pump. It hits you at the grocery store.

This tax is inflation. And it hits rich and poor alike. If politicians in Washington wanted to stop it, they could. Congress could fold the Federal Reserve. The president could order the Treasury to stop printing physical currency. But the lure of "easy money" and a managed economy promised by the Federal Reserve is too great.

We're told that this inflation isn't a concern. The Federal Reserve insists that their decisions to prop up asset values aren't leading to inflation. In fact, we're told that there's nothing wrong with a 2 to 3 percent inflation rate per year. Not only that, we're told that's a *good* thing, because it means we won't have *deflation*, the perceived evil of falling prices.

I guess central bankers never get a thrill buying something on sale!

In all seriousness, the Fed's policies couldn't be more destructive.

That's because inflation erodes the purchasing power of the dollar. But beyond that, it's the reason why *everything* — from shoes to groceries to gas to haircuts — costs more than it used to. Along the way, inflation has been so strong and pervasive that the government has taken the dollar off a gold backing, and adjusted the way inflation is measured to understate its effects.

A "Destruction Compounding" Machine

Most investors are familiar with the concept of compound interest. Albert Einstein is said to have called it "the most powerful force in the universe." Simply put, one dollar invested today, with the interest re-invested, performs substantially better than if you don't re-invest (more on that later).

Inflation is also a compounding force. Only rather than a force for good, it's a destruction-compounding machine. That's because the Federal Reserve targets 2 to 3 percent inflation annually. While that doesn't seem like much, over time it's quite destructive.

Over the past quarter century, for example, a period that included falling interest rates and a prolonged period of "low" inflation, the value of the dollar still fell by *half* — 50 percent. And that's according to the government-adjusted statistics.

Since 1971, when Nixon officially severed all ties that the dollar had to gold in the international markets (gold was still banned domestically), the dollar's purchasing power has plunged more than 80 percent.

The farther back your starting point, the greater destruction of purchasing power. In fact, what used to cost only $1 in 1870 now costs

United States Dollar

Dollar's purchasing power has plunged as currency circulation has exploded!

SOURCE: DollarDaze.org

more than $17 today. Look at the chart below. You'll see I'm not joking when I talk about the destructive tax of inflation:

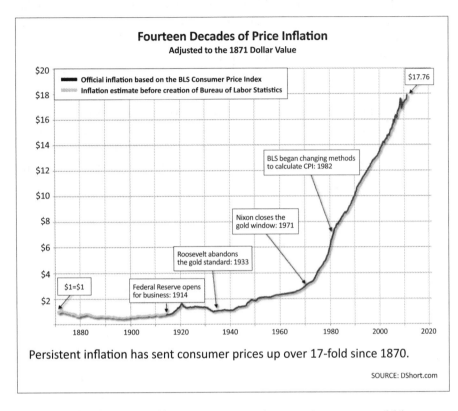

Fourteen Decades of Price Inflation
Adjusted to the 1871 Dollar Value

Official inflation based on the BLS Consumer Price Index

Inflation estimate before creation of Bureau of Labor Statistics

$17.76

BLS began changing methods to calculate CPI: 1982

Nixon closes the gold window: 1971

Roosevelt abandons the gold standard: 1933

$1=$1

Federal Reserve opens for business: 1914

Persistent inflation has sent consumer prices up over 17-fold since 1870.

SOURCE: DShort.com

Or, to look at it another way, a mere six cents in 1913 would buy one dollar's worth of goods today.

The sad irony is, this destruction of value couldn't have been made possible without the creation of the Federal Reserve and the abandonment of the gold standard. How is this ironic? One of the Fed's stated goals is to "foster price stability."

This goes beyond a simple "oops." The destruction of the dollar is clear. It likely won't stop anytime soon. For the average American looking to retire, it should be a big, red, burning flag.

It's clear the Fed has been too inflationary, especially for the last decade.

When measured in the performance of gold and silver, hard assets that *used* to back paper money, the decline of the dollar in the past 10 years has been *staggering*. Gold has surged from a low of $250 per ounce to more than $1,500. Silver has moved from a low of $5 to more than $48 per ounce.

To some investors, gold and silver make sense as long as interest rates are so low, since the metals themselves don't pay a dividend. Add in inflation rates greater than zero percent, and it's clear we haven't seen the top in precious metals prices yet.

That's because precious metals really aren't rising, it's the dollar that's falling.

As the dollar goes, so goes your prospect for a sound retirement in traditional, dollar-based retirement assets like bonds and annuities.

And, of course, the most relied-on retirement asset of all, housing, is still in the throes of a free-flowing, dollar-induced real estate bubble.

CHAPTER 2

Bankers, Can You Spare a McMansion?

More than 1 out of every 11 homes in America are vacant, and 28 percent of homeowners are "underwater" on their mortgage (owing more than the house is worth at the time of sale). Banks that have foreclosed have a "shadow inventory" of over 1 million homes to sell, but don't want to depress the market any further, lest they admit more losses.

Pick any statistic or factoid. The housing market is still an ugly mess.

The Case-Shiller Index, which tracks the largest housing markets in the country, is starting to trend down again after a modest bounce following massive government assistance to the banking and housing sector in 2009 (see chart on the following page).

Of course, some pullback is to be expected. At the height of the housing boom, banks were lending to anyone who asked for money. You could buy a million-dollar home via a so-called "NINJA" loan—meaning No Income, No Job or Assets.

Or, if you had a job, like the well-documented story of strawberry picker Alberto Ramirez, your $14,000 income could have qualified you to purchase a $720,000 home in Fresno, Calif.

Even before the bubble fully burst, that event was sure to raise some eyebrows.

It wasn't always this way, although part of the American dream was always predicated on home ownership.

The Federal government was always willing to lend a helping hand. The Homestead Act sent Americans west to settle the prairie and claim free land from the U.S. government. Mortgage terms went

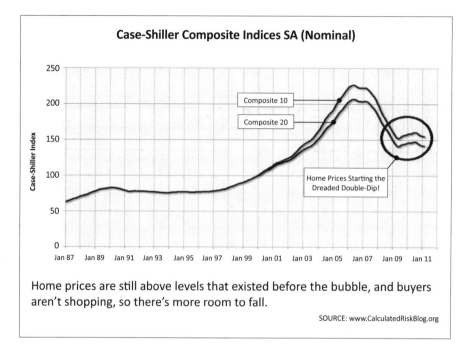

Case-Shiller Composite Indices SA (Nominal)

Composite 10

Composite 20

Home Prices Starting the Dreaded Double-Dip!

Home prices are still above levels that existed before the bubble, and buyers aren't shopping, so there's more room to fall.

SOURCE: www.CalculatedRiskBlog.org

from seven years with a balloon payment to 30 years to . . . much more exotic terms.

One such extreme was the negative amortization loan. Under this loan, interest payments were less than the minimum needed to pay down the principal and the total accrued interest, so the total balance outstanding on the loan actually grew each month!

Before the extremities of the bubble, homes provided a modest 1.8 percent historical return above interest. A family who lived in their home long enough to pay off the mortgage had a huge source of equity that they could use in retirement, either by selling the house, using a reverse mortgage, or even renting it out and downsizing to a condo in Florida.

During the bubble, many were seduced by the possibility of fast and easy gains in real estate. For those without retirement savings, it made sense to build a real estate empire. Start with one property, fix it, flip it, and repeat until you had dozens and could live off the cash flows.

Once television shows cropped up to follow around these budding real estate moguls, it was too late for any rational behavior in the real estate market. Plenty of folks without a background in real estate saw how easy (and profitable) it was to "flip" a home in a matter of days, weeks, or, in the worst-case scenario, months.

If only lending standards weren't so loose. If only a higher down payment was required. If only bankers had been, well, responsible bankers. They could have followed the old 3-6-3 rule in banking: borrow at 3 percent, lend at 6 percent, and hit the golf course at 3 p.m.

Alas, the bankers were greedy too. They received fat origination fees, the possibility for refinance fees down the line, and the ability to send any bad mortgage they created off to Wall Street to have it sliced and diced into an AAA-rated debt instrument.

Unlike stocks, which quickly bounced back from their lows, real estate prices have been hovering for over a year — and by some measures are declining again!

Any way you slice it, the real estate market, a key source of retirement security for millions of Americans, is still down for the count. It still will be until all those bad debts are cleared off the table.

Sad as it is, America's housing debt is *nothing* compared to the federal government.

And, it's going to get worse before it gets better, because America's growing debt problems could permanently lower our standard of living on a much bigger level than the bursting of the housing bubble.

CHAPTER 3

One Nation, Under Massive Debt, With Spending and Entitlements for All

The Federal Reserve doesn't operate in a vacuum. Perpetual money creation is tied to our bloated federal government, and a federal debt that now exceeds $15 trillion — nearly double the amount it was in 2005 (see chart on the following page).

Several factors have contributed to this massive spending. The largest factors going into the budget deficits of the past decade have been automatic increases in spending on welfare programs like Social Security and Medicare. Ongoing operations in Afghanistan and Iraq cost billions per year as well.

As the economy was still rising, however, tax revenues continued to increase. This changed substantially when housing prices stopped rising. As jobs were lost, government lost income taxes on those jobs, and started paying out more in unemployment benefits. Individuals with stock losses were able to start writing off losses on their tax returns rather than pay capital gains.

Thanks to this crisis, with only $2 trillion brought in through taxes each year, the government's debt is effectively seven times its annual "income."

I'd say that the government spends like a drunken sailor, but even a drunken sailor doesn't run up debts more than seven times his annual salary!

But billions and trillions are numbers that are difficult to really grasp. They're so high that, to many Americans, it's not even worth thinking about. So let's break this ballooning debt down into each individual's share.

Our government spends so much that every man, woman, and

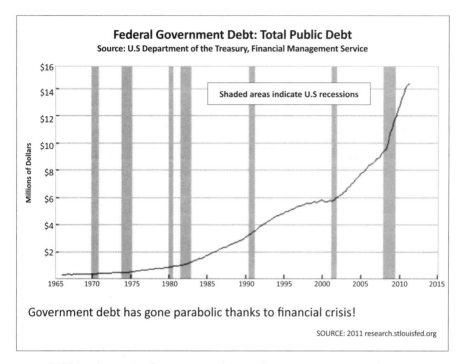

Federal Government Debt: Total Public Debt
Source: U.S Department of the Treasury, Financial Management Service

Shaded areas indicate U.S recessions

Government debt has gone parabolic thanks to financial crisis!

SOURCE: 2011 research.stlouisfed.org

child in the United States would need to pony up more than $35,000 to pay it off. That's just the most recent data through the end of 2009 (see chart on the following page).

Since 2009, the 111th Congress, held between 2009 and early 2011, added over $3.2 *trillion* to this debt — more than the first 100 sessions of Congress *combined*. Unofficial estimates place the debt per person at over $48,000 per year. That's more than the average employee makes in a year!

Not only is the United States spending more than ever, it's doing so at a greater rate. It's no wonder the Fed needs to keep interest rates at zero! If rates were higher, it would cost hundreds of billions more to simply make the interest payments on our national debt.

America's debt payments in fiscal year 2011 amounted to a whopping $244,476,372,569.22, according to the Treasury.

Remember: Most government debt is in short-term securities that are simply "rolled over." These rates on short-term debt are well under 2 to 3 percent. At a higher interest rate, say 5 percent, all taxes would eventually go toward the interest payments on our debt alone!

Unfortunately, there's no plan in America to reverse course and undo the damage that's being done. Interest rates are set to remain at

0 to 0.25 percent through mid-2012, according to the Federal Reserve.

The only recent compromise involved *cutting* 2 percent of Social Security taxes, and saving $30 billion in other programs. That's chump change. The failure of the "Super Committee" to reach an agreement simply ensures that future spending will simply grow at a slower rate.

If anything, these short-sighted decisions will only make the problem worse when things finally explode. For now, we're stuck with a batch of politicians that are like ostriches: Their heads are in the sand.

These measures of our debt overlook one major area that's being swept under the rug: the true costs of entitlement spending, namely Social Security and Medicare. As Social Security is akin to a retirement program, let's take a closer look to see how America's pension plan is holding up.

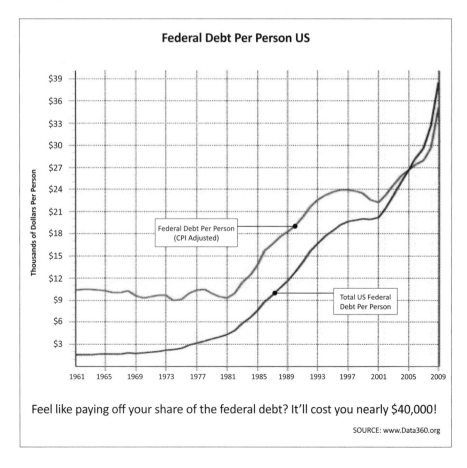

Federal Debt Per Person US

Feel like paying off your share of the federal debt? It'll cost you nearly $40,000!

SOURCE: www.Data360.org

CHAPTER 4

Social Insecurity: America's Pension Plan Currently Running in the Red

Economists estimate that 40 percent of Americans over age 65 rely entirely on Social Security for their income. That's shocking, since the program has always been designed to supplement pensions, savings, and other retirement income.

It also tells us that the system is creating a bizarre disincentive: Workers assume that the program will be sufficient for their retirement, so they no longer see the need to provide for other sources of retirement income.

That 40 percent is tightrope walking above a very fragile set of assumptions, namely that current payout levels will stay the same (including inflation adjustments). That might not be the case. According to the Government Accountability Office (GAO), Social Security has been running at a deficit since 2009, as high unemployment has lowered the total taxes paid into the system.

Without any changes to benefits or taxes, the program wasn't expected to reach a deficit until 2018. Due to this accelerated timetable, most estimates of the program's solvency are now entirely inaccurate.

With the estimates we do have, though, it's clear that the off-budget items on Social Security and Medicare are currently accruing liabilities of anywhere from $30 to $100 trillion, with most credible estimates lying in the $80 to $90 trillion range.

The program has run at a deficit since the start of the financial crisis, in 2008 and that doesn't look to change anytime soon. Instead, President Obama has pushed for tax relief on Social Security to get workers spending more again. However, that money is going to pay down current debt, rather than save for retirement.

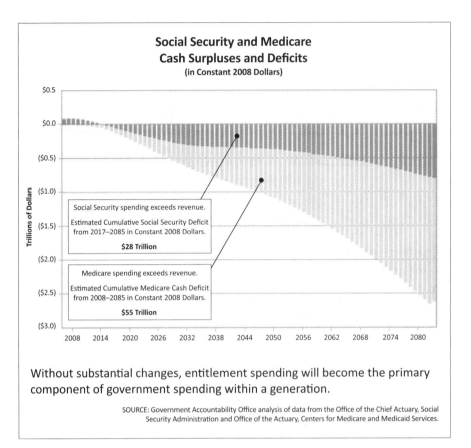

Social Security and Medicare Cash Surpluses and Deficits
(in Constant 2008 Dollars)

Social Security spending exceeds revenue.

Estimated Cumulative Social Security Deficit from 2017–2085 in Constant 2008 Dollars.

$28 Trillion

Medicare spending exceeds revenue.

Estimated Cumulative Medicare Cash Deficit from 2008–2085 in Constant 2008 Dollars.

$55 Trillion

Without substantial changes, entitlement spending will become the primary component of government spending within a generation.

SOURCE: Government Accountability Office analysis of data from the Office of the Chief Actuary, Social Security Administration and Office of the Actuary, Centers for Medicare and Medicaid Services.

Meanwhile, America continues to age. The baby boomers have started to reach retirement age. Longer life spans mean longer retirements. (Fact: The average life expectancy was 62 when the program was started, meaning more than half of those who paid into the program wouldn't reach 65 to receive benefits. Today's life expectancy is 78, meaning the average person can expect 13 years of benefits.) That's partially why the number of workers supporting retirees has declined from 40 to 1 to the order of 3 to 1.

Three solutions exist. Either benefits decline, taxes rise, or the system is privatized. The first two options will deal a major blow to economic growth. If benefits decline, seniors will have less disposable income to spend on economic growth. If taxes rise, working consumers won't be able to spend as much either.

As for the third option, we have to go south of the border to see how it works in action.

May 1, 2011 marked the 30th anniversary of the privatization of Chile's retirement program. By any account, it's been a wild success.

Chile mandates that workers pay 10 percent of their income into private accounts (much like a 401(k) program), rather than paying 12.4 percent into government coffers as Social Security does. While Social Security funds go into a pool to pay current retirees and invest any surplus in Treasurys earning anywhere from 1 to 2 percent, Chileans have options among various conservatively managed investment programs.

As a result, savers in Chile see a return of more than 9 percent per year, as opposed to the 1 to 2 percent return that current retirees in the U.S. are seeing over and above their initial contributions. (Future returns will be substantially lower, given the demographic shift to a larger retired population.)

Even better for Chileans: Their retirement accounts are personal property. So benefits can't be reduced or arbitrarily changed by government fiat.

In 2005, one journalist who ran the numbers found that under Social Security, he'd be entitled to $18,000 per year. While paying in less for Chile's program, he would be entitled to an annuity of $53,000 per year, *plus* a lump sum of $223,000.

That's why you need to do what American politicians won't: Create your own Chilean-style retirement plan.

It will require some creativity. At the moment, your "typical" retirement assets just won't give you the kind of returns you need due to today's ultra-low interest rates.

These Investments Have Limited Upside at Today's Low Rates!

- It's prudent to keep at least six months' worth of living expenses in a savings account, where it can be easily reached in an emergency. But, most savings accounts today offer interest rates anywhere from 0 to 1 percent. As a tool for retirement savings, it's akin to a blunt ax: ineffective.

- Bank certificates of deposits (CDs) offer slightly better yields, but in exchange investors lose liquidity. If money is needed and the CD is cashed in early, interest penalties apply.

- Treasury bonds are practically in bubble territory. Most issues trade near or above par, offering historically low yields, after a 30-year bull run. While short-term bonds may make the best investment as an alternative to holding cash, it's tough to argue that U.S. government bonds should constitute a core portfolio holding for income-oriented investors.

- Annuities can vary wildly in terms of the payout. While their greatest advantage lies in a fixed payout, the amount of capital locked up is substantial, and might not perform well in the event of inflation.

These cash-equivalents are low risk. But they offer such a low return at today's interest rates that investors will lose out after adjusting for inflation.

But that doesn't mean you're powerless against this hidden tax. There are ways to profit over and above inflation. And, it all starts with income.

PART

two

Why Income Investments Are the Key to Retirement Success

CHAPTER 5

Income: The Largest Factor in Investment Success

"Do you know the only thing that gives me pleasure? It's to see my dividends coming in." — John Rockefeller

Income has always been the key to making money in investments throughout history.

Don't get me wrong — appreciation is great too. There's nothing like speculating on a stock, being right, and banking profits of several hundred to several thousand percent. But, you can't count on being able to persistently make those kinds of gains. For every "10 bagger," the stock that rises tenfold, there are the stocks that don't go anywhere, decline, or go bankrupt.

Ultimately, preserving capital is key for reaching retirement goals. As you get older and closer to retirement, the last thing you want to do is risk your money on the next big thing, only to see it blow up. In fact, a great way to think of risk is the likelihood of permanent loss of capital. By owning assets that produce income, you lower the risk substantially compared to chasing the latest "fad" stock.

In the days before the 1929 market crash that brought about the SEC and other regulations, investors looking at stocks relied *entirely* on the income. They demanded higher dividend yields than seen in markets today. Indeed, early stocks often had a set par value, and were more often bought for the high dividends than capital appreciation.

Why? Because the regular payout of cash to shareholders proved that a company really brought in cash to begin with.

That's a huge contrast when compared to today's stock-chasers, looking for fat capital gains and little, if any, dividends. Since the great

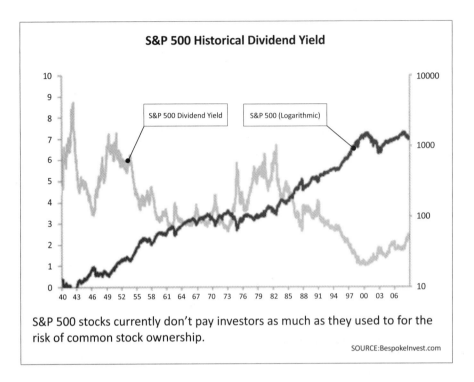

S&P 500 Historical Dividend Yield

S&P 500 Dividend Yield

S&P 500 (Logarithmic)

S&P 500 stocks currently don't pay investors as much as they used to for the risk of common stock ownership.

SOURCE:BespokeInvest.com

stock market bull run began in 1980, the average dividend yield on the S&P 500 has dropped from 6 percent to under 2 percent today.

When fast-moving stocks get crushed, those investors see their portfolios get creamed if they didn't take enough profits off the table during the run-up. Of course, that doesn't take into account that some of those big profits might go into the next company to go bankrupt!

There's a substantially better way to consistently make money in stocks than chase the markets. This was confirmed in a groundbreaking study made by Wharton School of Economics professor Jeremy Siegel.

In his 1994 book *Stocks for the Long Run*, Siegel's research showed that over a long enough time period, the returns on stocks with the dividends reinvested beat every other asset class hands down.

For his follow-up book, *The Future for Investors*, Siegel examined the individual stocks in the S&P 500 that had the best performance since the late 1950s. His results were *astonishing*.

Due to the power of reinvested income from dividends, the best-performing stocks in the S&P 500 were the "stodgy" companies in the index that were never replaced with high-flying growth companies.

The best-performing stock was tobacco producer Philip Morris (now Altria Group, ticker MO), with nearly 20 percent annual returns. That includes a period where tobacco stocks were hit with multibillion-dollar lawsuits, saw their advertising banned, and were vilified more than banks are today!

The primary reason for Philip Morris' amazing return in spite of these headwinds was the reinvestment of dividends. Philip Morris continued to raise its dividends annually, so when the price was slammed from tobacco litigation, each dividend payment would buy more shares (or fractions of shares) than it would have at a higher price.

This left investors with a substantial number of shares, each spinning off ever-rising dividend income. As Siegel says, "Although the earnings, sales, and even market values of the new firms grew faster than those of the older firms, the price investors paid for these stocks was simply too high to generate good returns. These higher prices meant lower dividend yields and therefore, fewer shares accumulated through reinvesting dividends."

A few other stocks performed almost as well as the tobacco producer. Siegel found that the top 20 highest-returning companies in the original S&P 500 were dominated from the consumer staples, pharmaceuticals, and energy sectors.

Replicate Siegel's Research With Dividend Growth Stocks

For investors with a long-term outlook and who don't need current income, the best approach to building a large pool of retirement income is to find quality, dividend-paying stocks, and reinvest the capital for a prolonged period.

Investors who focus on companies with a history of growing their dividends over time will do even better when it comes time to stop reinvesting and start living off the dividends. This is especially true for tax-deferred accounts, where the 15 percent tax rate on dividends doesn't come into play.

Many lists are available online showing companies that have increased their dividends annually. Studying these lists shows a few key differences between a dividend grower and other types of companies:

- First, the company has a "moat." That means it has some kind of advantage over its competitors. Wal-Mart's distribution system gives it an advantage over other retailers. Kraft's brands are more trusted than lesser-known food products. Coke's flavor and bottling network can't be replicated by a startup today. It can even include intellectual property, like IBM, a company that creates hundreds of new patents each year.

- Second, the company needs to generate substantial cash-flow. These are the types of companies that *benefit* from recessions and credit crunches. They've got the balance sheets to stay in business and even expand when their weaker competitors go out of business. A company that can consistently bring in large amounts of cash also has the financial reserves available to pay out dividends every year.

- Third, the company has a parasitic relationship with inflation. What do I mean by that? It's simple. The company has the power to raise prices and pass higher inflationary costs onto their consumers. Whether it's a service company like Automatic Data Processing, or a consumer goods producer like McDonald's or Hershey's, when prices go up, they can respond with price increases (or in the case of consumer-goods makers, decrease the quantity of their product per serving).

It's no surprise that companies meeting these simple criteria for dividend growth are well-known, large-cap household names. These companies know they can't rapidly grow the size of their business like they have in the past, so they now focus on paying a dividend.

And, as we've seen from Siegel's research, reinvesting these dividends is the key to higher returns, even if the share price moves nowhere. It also explains why so many of the common stocks held by Warren Buffett's Berkshire Hathaway are dividend-paying blue chips.

Three companies meeting the above criteria look like a good place to start a dividend-growth-oriented portfolio today. Two are well-known to income investors, and the third is an up-and-coming dividend player in an unlikely sector.

Their current dividend yields are nothing to write home about (especially compared to most of the stocks in this report). But the power of compounding and rising dividends over time could provide investors with opportunities to substantially increase their wealth before retirement.

CHAPTER 6

Three Dividend Giants Safe for Income

Safe Income Payout #1:
A Healthcare Giant Built for Dividend Reinvestment

The first dividend stock won't come as a surprise to any value investor. It's a core holding in the Berkshire Hathaway portfolio. But it's also one of the 10 individual stocks that Warren Buffett owns *outside* his stake in Berkshire. In fact, he likes it so much he owns over four million shares.

It's none other than Johnson & Johnson (JNJ).

The company's products range from brand-name pharmaceuticals to medical devices and equipment all the way down to baby powder and Band-Aids. It's a global giant that just celebrated its 125th anniversary.

But, bad news is hitting J&J from all over. U.S. sales have been flat since 2007. The company has had to recall products. Two of its top drugs, Levaquin and Concerta, are reaching the end of their patent life. And, the company is saturated with lawsuits across all its divisions.

In other words, the company faces significant headwinds and low prospects for growth. That tends to keep the price low — and the dividend yield high.

That's a bid odd for a company with an amazing balance sheet: Johnson & Johnson is one of only four companies in the world to sport an AAA credit rating. The company also expanded sales by 14 percent in emerging markets in 2010.

On April 28, 2011, J&J increased its dividend 5.6 percent to $0.57 per share, giving the company an annual yield of 3.7 percent. The company has raised its dividend every year since 1963. It has recently

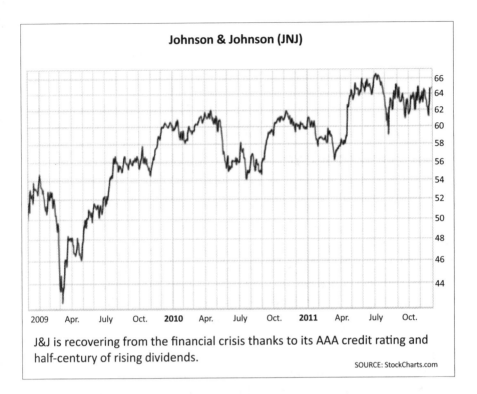

Johnson & Johnson (JNJ)

J&J is recovering from the financial crisis thanks to its AAA credit rating and half-century of rising dividends.

SOURCE: StockCharts.com

broken through a pre-market crash high, but remains well off the premium markets placed on it 10 years ago.

With its robust global growth, trusted brand names, and healthy balance sheet, Johnson & Johnson is one stock that investors can tuck away to reinvest the dividends for years to come. With a history of rising dividends, it's also one of the few common stocks that can provide current income with a higher payout in the future.

Safe Income Payout #2:
North America's Top Food Producer Is Dishing Out the Income

This company's products are well-known in every grocery store and kitchen in the United States, and increasingly the world. They include Nabisco, Oreo, Maxwell House, Oscar Mayer . . . and far more (40 of its brands are over 100 years old). Add a recent major acquisition, and you've got a food company with a bigger exposure to confectionaries than Hershey.

It's none other than Kraft Foods (KFT), a cash-flow king and global powerhouse. Shares have followed the market up over the past two years, only recently breaking through pre-crash highs.

Earnings took a hit following its large acquisition of Cadbury, but the effects of the acquisition are already starting to show up on the company's income statement. For patient investors, Kraft's 3.4 percent dividend yield offers a substantial return over fixed-income investments, backed by the earning power of a well-branded food company.

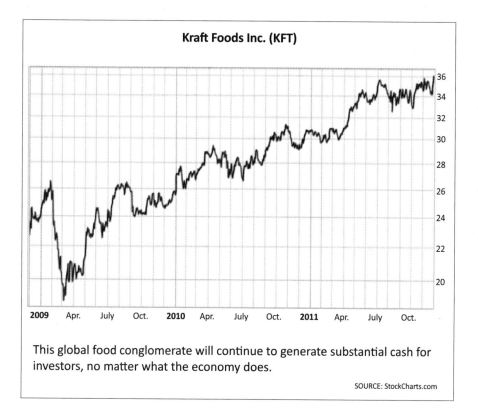

Kraft Foods Inc. (KFT)

This global food conglomerate will continue to generate substantial cash for investors, no matter what the economy does.

SOURCE: StockCharts.com

The company has more than doubled its dividend since 2001, bringing quarterly payments to $0.29 per share.

While most investors deride Kraft as a slow-moving behemoth, it's a clear-cut value play. It should be no surprise that Kraft is another of the very select few stocks that Warren Buffett owns outside his Berkshire Hathaway holdings (yes, even after the company sold shares of Kraft in 2010 to help fund the purchase of Burlington Northern).

Safe Income Payout #3:

A Value Play in a Surprising Place: A Key Player In Internet Infrastructure

As one of today's most unloved companies, Cisco Systems (CSCO) looks like an astute purchase for any value-oriented investor. Why? Because it's a major global player and sports a fortress-like balance sheet that would make Warren Buffett envious.

Free cash flow has more than doubled from 4.1 billion to 9.2 billion in the past 10 years. In that time, management has reduced the number of shares outstanding by 22 percent — from 7.4 billion to 5.84 billion. The company paid its first dividend on April 20.

Meanwhile, it trades at a PE of 12.8, substantially below its historical average of 20.4. Back out the company's net cash position of $39 billion, and the metrics look even more alluring.

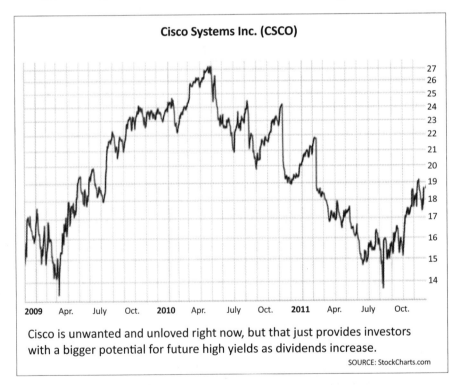

Cisco Systems Inc. (CSCO)

Cisco is unwanted and unloved right now, but that just provides investors with a bigger potential for future high yields as dividends increase.

SOURCE: StockCharts.com

If you wanted to grab Cisco's market share, you'd need more than the $96 billion it's currently going for.

While not on the scale of McDonald's or Coke, Cisco has built a reputation over other players in the industry. It's tough to make the argument that there can be a brand moat with a tech company, since new developments lead to lower prices and better products. But Cisco comes pretty close.

Cisco's networking technology enables everything from basic Web browsing to Internet video conferencing. It's effectively the concrete of the information superhighway. Nevertheless, shares are a staggering 84 percent off the company's all-time high in 2000.

With markets seeing increased volatility, Cisco's moat is protecting shares from falling. Global franchises rarely get this cheap. The company's recently introduced dividend gives the stock an effective yield of 1.4 percent. It also represents less than 20 percent of earnings, meaning there's room for further dividend increases down the line, even if the company's growth grinds to a halt.

A technology stock might not seem like the most logical choice for a dividend growth stock, especially one so recent. But, Cisco is following a path set by big-cap tech names like Microsoft and Intel when their growth rates started slowing. Both those companies have upped their dividends over time. It's likely Cisco will too.

BONUS Safe Income Payout #4:
A Fat Yield on a Perpetually Unloved Common Stock

Most common stocks simply won't provide investors with a high enough stream of current income the moment they're purchased. While a 2 to 3 percent yield is certainly better than cash under the mattress or in the bank, it's nowhere near the 4 percent that most retirement planners advise their clients to be able to safely pull out each year.

The best thing investors should do with common stocks is allow them time to compound. Decades would be ideal, but for anyone approaching retirement massively underfunded, higher-yielding stocks are needed.

So, with a current yield at a fat 6.0 percent, investors may want to take a closer look at Altria Group (MO).

While not as cheap as it was during the heyday of tobacco litigation in the 1990s, margins remain healthy and the company remains profitable in a world where the company can't advertise its primary product! Profit margins are 24 percent; return on equity is 82 percent.

These are the kind of profit margins that make a high-flying tech company like Apple envious. But it's really simple why. Tobacco products are cheap to make, are sold at a substantially higher price to addicts, and the government (both state and federal) reaps huge taxes per pack.

More importantly, the dividend has substantially increased over the years, even accounting for the spinoff of Philip Morris International. Investors who need current income and are willing to risk the short-term gyrations of the stock market couldn't do much better than owning some shares of Altria.

Altria Group Inc. (MO)

Altria's returns since the financial crisis have had substantially less volatility than the average stock. That's a key feature to help dividend investors sleep well at night.

SOURCE: StockCharts.com

It's no surprise that Altria is a dividend titan, even after being listed by Jeremy Siegel as the best-performing stock since the inception of the S&P 500.

But he's not the only one noting the company's performance to shareholders. In 2007, it was revealed that Federal Reserve Chairman Ben Bernanke had his entire portfolio *solely in Altria stock*.

I'd consider that a strong endorsement that Altria's products stand a good chance of outperforming Bernanke's monetary mayhem.

Alternative Sources of Income Outside of Common Stocks

For investors with a long-term outlook, safe dividend stocks with a history of dividend growth can work. But for investors closer to retirement, the kind of income offered from these companies might not cut it.

That's where alternative asset classes and off-the-radar investments come into play. The next part of this report deals with those companies, and how they can provide you with higher yields. Some of them have bond-like qualities that offer a lower risk of capital loss than stocks. But, like any investment, there are risks involved.

These alternatives range from alternative income-generating strategies, to becoming a passive landlord, to becoming a miniature oil baron to being the bank's banker. Most of these assets also feature a slightly different tax structure, so you'll need to review these investments with your financial adviser and accountant as to where they are best suited in your investment portfolio.

Typically, the biggest difference between these alternative assets and cash, bonds, and common stock is that they have less liquidity. In many cases, this isn't a problem if you're investing for higher income. But, I want you to be fully aware of both the benefits and the potential perils of an investment before you decide to allocate a single dollar.

Each high-income investment is a little different, so we'll take them one at a time, and look at a few companies in each category that may be worthy of your investment dollars.

CHAPTER 7

Become a Landowner Without the Hassle: Real Estate Investment Trusts

If any two words might be considered dirty in today's investment environment, they are "real estate." That holds especially true for small investors who bought and tried to "flip" properties quickly for a fast, tidy profit.

There are some advantages to real estate for investors. First, with the use of a mortgage, investors can employ leverage. For example, using a $100,000 grubstake, investors can purchase a $500,000 property.

Of course, what most appealed to investors during the housing bubble was that nowhere near a 20 percent down payment was needed! For borrowers who had a respectable down payment and focused on the cash-flow aspects of real estate, the investment returns have been much more consistent than for those who invested strictly with a fast resale in mind.

Add the hassle of finding tenants, making repairs, paying bills, and it appears that today's real estate market isn't optimal for most small investors, even if the property can bring in cash each month outside the mortgage payment and other expenses.

Fortunately, a corporate structure that came into being in 1960 can offer individual investors access to the real estate markets without the hassle of being a landlord. These corporations are called Real Estate Investment Trusts.

A REIT is pretty straightforward. It's a type of corporation designed to "pass through" 90 percent of the income on to its shareholders. By doing so, the REIT avoids corporate taxes. Individual investors are usually taxed at their ordinary rates of income for REIT distributions (usually higher than the 15 percent tax rate currently on the books).

There's a downside to this structure. To raise money for future acquisitions, a REIT must either take on massive amounts of debt, which can threaten the dividend, or issue more shares, which dilutes the value for existing shareholders.

Since REITs are designed for income investors and no single investor is allowed to own more than 5 percent of the outstanding shares, such dilutions are typically small to keep the share price from taking a big plunge in the first place.

REITs can include anything from mortgage notes to physical homes and office buildings. Some focus on one small geographic area or investment type, while others are much broader. This diversity provides some excellent opportunities.

Three REIT picks for those needing current high income include a monthly dividend player in commercial real estate, a trust tied to a growing demographic trend, and a yield-hog that should continue to deliver fat returns as long as interest rates don't move.

High Income Payout #1:
"Our Prototypical Shareholder Is a 70-Year-Old Retired School Teacher"

Realty Income (O) is so focused on its monthly payments to investors that it registered the phrase "The Monthly Dividend Company ®."

But, that doesn't mean the company is leveraged up to the hilt to support its 5.4 percent dividend. The company does NOT use mortgages to purchase the 2,500 properties it owns in 49 states.

This lower leverage keeps the dividend secure from potential cuts, which many REITs were forced to do during the credit crunch. In fact, Realty Income has even managed to raise its dividend since 2007, from $0.126 per month to $0.145 per month.

Sounds pretty stodgy, right? Take a look at how Realty Income has performed in the past three years:

Compared to the overall markets, since inception with the dividends reinvested, Realty Income has left nearly every other real estate play in the dust.

There's another secret to Realty Income's success: **They're a lazy landlord**.

Let me explain. Most of their tenants, including big names like Taco Bell, PetSmart, Coca-Cola, and Diageo, have "triple-net leases" with Realty Income. That means the tenants are responsible for any

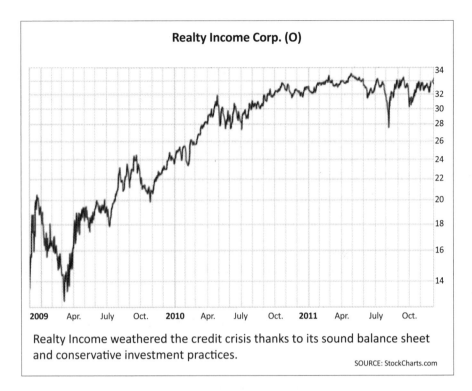

Realty Income Corp. (O)

Realty Income weathered the credit crisis thanks to its sound balance sheet and conservative investment practices.

SOURCE: StockCharts.com

maintenance, taxes, and the like on the property.

Realty Income just collects the rent. It doesn't need an army of maintenance people; it doesn't have to deal with property tax or building insurance paperwork. Its $4.45 billion empire is run with a meager staff of 79. Any company that can keep its corporate expenses low has a tremendous advantage to shareholders.

Typically, Realty Income likes lease terms of 20 years. Of course, that's a double-edged sword. Realty Income won't be able to raise rates as much as other property owners might be able to, even though they do have provisions in their contracts to make inflation adjustments.

Realty Income is a perfect SWAN stock for income investors: Backed by a diverse portfolio of major commercial tenants, investors can collect monthly income and Sleep Well at Night.

High Income Payout #2:

A High-Yielding Play on the "Graying" of America

While most parts of the real estate market remain a major concern, investors looking at America's long-term demographics have been making bets that one small subset of REITs will perform well. These REITs, which play off the trend of America's aging population, own medical facilities, nursing homes, and assisted care facilities.

Following the demographics is always a trend worth investing in. Investors in the 1950s would have done well to follow the baby boomers by investing in companies like Johnson & Johnson for their baby products, or Procter & Gamble for their diapers. In the 1960s, it would have been toy company Mattel or restaurant chain McDonald's. In the 1980s, investing in financial companies would have paid off substantially as boomers started saving and investing.

That's why today, in addition to investing in a healthcare company like Johnson & Johnson, income-oriented investors should look to healthcare REITs.

In this space, one of the best-of-breed plays is Long Term Care (LTC). LTC invests in over 210 skilled nursing properties and assisted living facilities in 30 states, either through direct ownership or mortgages. Only one state, Texas, accounts for more than 10 percent of the company's geographic exposure.

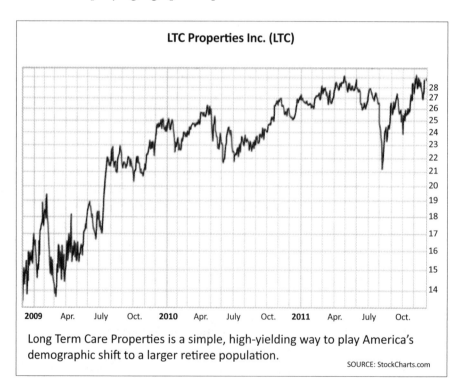

Long Term Care Properties is a simple, high-yielding way to play America's demographic shift to a larger retiree population.

SOURCE: StockCharts.com

This $750 million market cap company sports under $90 million in net debt, giving it a healthy balance sheet. The monthly dividend yield is 6.3 percent, and the company has grown the dividend 158 percent since 2003, after adjusting for stock splits.

At the time of this report, shares were in a short-term downtrend, but were in a larger-term uptrend.

In the REIT space, LTC has underperformed the market in the past year, but in the past five years has returned 80 percent (including the dividend) compared to a 15 percent return on the S&P 500 index.

The company expects this outperformance to continue, noting that the 70- and 80-plus age groups are projected to grow at three times the rate of the general population of the United States over the next 20 years. Increased Medicare spending on nursing homes makes this company poised to profit from increased entitlement spending as well.

High Income Payout #3:

Borrowing Low and Lending High: One REIT Poised to Profit From Low Interest Rates

The 5 percent yields on Realty Income and Long Term Care are certainly nothing to sneeze at. But, for our final REIT, let's look at one with a higher risk profile, and, consequently a higher yield. How much higher?

Try a fat 15.1 percent.

There's a big catch to investors of Annaly Mortgage (NLY). Interest rates need to stay low for a long period of time for the returns to add up. But with the Fed's commitment to keeping rates near zero percent through mid-2012, Annaly could have a substantial payoff in any income portfolio.

Annaly needs low interest rates because the company invests in mortgage debt. It borrows at those ultra-low short-term rates, to buy government-backed mortgage debt yielding higher rates. By doing so, it earns a "spread" between the rates. If it borrows at 1 percent, for instance, and buys a portfolio of mortgages with a yield of 6 percent, the spread is 5 percent.

Thanks to the company's REIT structure, 90 percent of the cash flows from that spread are passed on to investors.

It's important to note that the company's dividend can be erratic, and that the company also survived the credit crunch relatively unscathed, thanks to its loan portfolio of government-backed securities.

Looking back over a five-year period, the company has traded in a range between $8 and $21, making Annaly a better play for those who need current income rather than those looking to reinvest dividends.

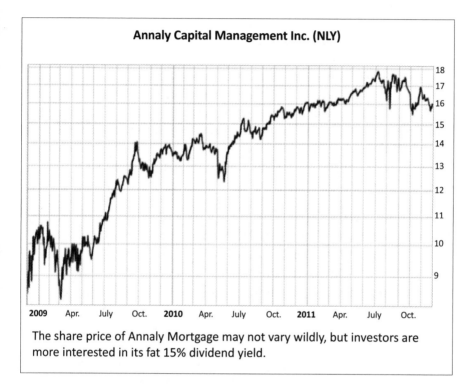

Annaly Capital Management Inc. (NLY)

The share price of Annaly Mortgage may not vary wildly, but investors are more interested in its fat 15% dividend yield.

Annaly is effectively a leveraged play on low interest rates. At the first sign of an aggressive increase in interest rates, investors will need to exit their position. But even with that caveat and the company's leverage, the substantial dividend outweighs the current risk in today's low-interest rate environment.

CHAPTER 8

Build Wealth the Rockefeller Way and Use the Corporate Structure That Pipelines Use

Adjusted for inflation, John D. Rockefeller's $318 billion net worth would make Bill Gates, Warren Buffett, or Carlos Slim look like paupers. Even without adjusting for inflation, he was America's first billionaire.

How did he do it? With the creation of Standard Oil, the conglomerate of oil production facilities, properties, and pipelines.

Of course, there were some mistakes along the way. Rockefeller started by shipping oil through tanker cars on trains, before stumbling on the more efficient system of pipelines. Bypassing the railroads was such a huge cost savings that his original pipelines had armed guards to keep railroad companies from sabotaging this critical infrastructure.

Any company looking to ship oil or natural gas today has to use pipelines as well, making them akin to a "toll booth" industry. Operators run the infrastructure and charge for its use, but they don't own the underlying commodity being shipped. That's a great, steady source of revenue in today's world of volatile energy prices.

Today, most pipelines in the United States are owned by a type of structure designed for pass-through benefits similar to a real estate investment trust.

They're called Master Limited Partnerships (MLPs).

They offer pass-through income, typically on natural resource infrastructure such as pipelines. Yields on the distributions to partners tend to run in the 5 to 8 percent range.

They also offer the benefit of pass-through depreciation. Companies routinely "write down" the value of an asset as it's used up. MLP owners can "write off" on their tax return part of the depreciation of an MLP's asset — meaning their fat yields are also bolstered by lower reportable income during tax time.

Because of this "write off" feature, MLPs aren't the best choice for your tax-deferred accounts like your 401(k) or IRA. Since taxes in these accounts are deferred, you won't be able to take advantage of the depreciation. It's best to hold MLPs in a regular brokerage account, where you can still use the depreciation to offset taxes on capital gains and dividends.

On the tax front, a K-1 form is issued at the end of each year instead of the traditional 1099 to track the distributions and depreciation. While some deride this extra paperwork as a nightmare, it only takes a few extra minutes when preparing tax returns.

One word of caution: MLPs are a hot sector.

In 2010, we saw the creation of the first funds and ETFs that focus exclusively on MLPs. As these funds got off the ground, their buying activity moved up prices across the entire sector. Shares have pulled back a bit once the buying stopped, but it's possible that there will be more volatility going forward as new funds enter the marketplace.

With that in mind, let's look at three of the top companies in this sector.

MLP Opportunity #1:
The Blue-Chip of MLPs: Kinder Morgan
As a spinoff of Enron, it's easy to argue that Kinder Morgan Pipelines (KMP) got some of the company's best assets. That's because Kinder Morgan is the largest independent transporter of petroleum products, the largest terminal operator, and the second-largest transporter of natural gas in the U.S.

While some MLPs own oil and gas wells, Kinder Morgan's focus on pipelines gives it a stability of revenue that isn't necessarily dependent on the price of oil and gas. In other words, it's an energy play in the sense that more oil and gas will flow at higher prices, but the company isn't completely tied to the commodity price. They're paid strictly for the quantity shipped.

The current yield on Kinder Morgan is 6.1 percent. The company has a solid history of increasing the distribution, and another increase is expected in 2011.

The company is expanding pipeline operations to take advantage of natural gas opportunities in the Marcellus shale region of West

Virginia and Pennsylvania. In short, investors in this blue-chip of MLPs get a high current income, along with favorable growth prospects in the future of natural gas.

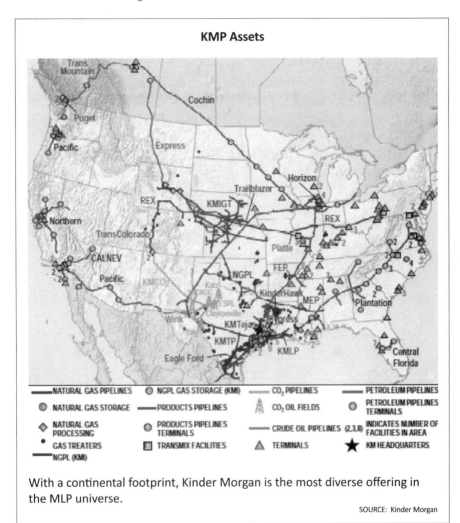

KMP Assets

With a continental footprint, Kinder Morgan is the most diverse offering in the MLP universe.

SOURCE: Kinder Morgan

Just like a blue-chip company, Kinder Morgan tends to be pricier than its peers in the MLP space. That's understandable given the company's geographic diversity and size of its assets relative to other pipeline companies.

If there's one company worth paying up for to obtain higher quality, it's Kinder Morgan.

MLP Opportunity #2:

An Up-and-Comer With Growth Potential: Buckeye Partners

Buckeye Partners (BPL) isn't as large or as well-known as Kinder Morgan, but it is currently expanding through a major acquisition that makes it an up-and-comer.

Unlike Kinder Morgan, which operates entirely independently, Buckeye operates and maintains pipelines owned by major oil and chemical companies. That's in addition to the 5,400 miles of pipeline it owns, as well as natural gas storage facilities and an ammonia pipeline.

Buckeye is currently on track to acquire over 30 terminals and over 1,000 miles of pipeline from BP. These assets are concentrated on the East Coast and Midwest, with a large portion in Ohio.

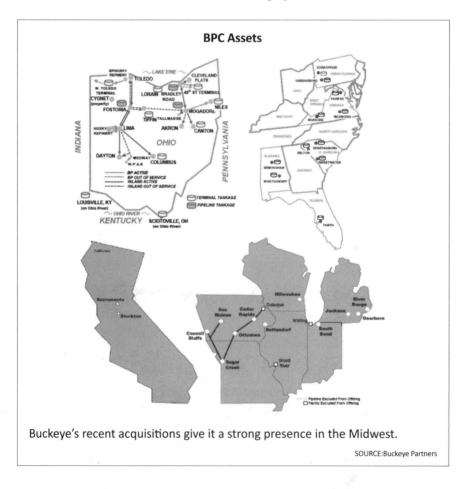

BPC Assets

Buckeye's recent acquisitions give it a strong presence in the Midwest.

SOURCE: Buckeye Partners

Like Kinder Morgan, it's geographically diverse. Unlike Kinder Morgan, Buckeye operates both as an owner and a service provider. Either way, it pays for unit holders. Buckeye yields 6.6 percent.

Out of the entire MLP universe, Buckeye Partners has the longest streak when it comes to paying distributions, currently at 16 years.

MLP Opportunity #3:

Long-Term, Value-Oriented Management: Boardwalk Pipeline Partners

Operating in a smaller geographic region and focusing on natural gas transmission, there is one key advantage that sets Boardwalk Pipeline (BWP) apart from other MLPs: its value-oriented management team.

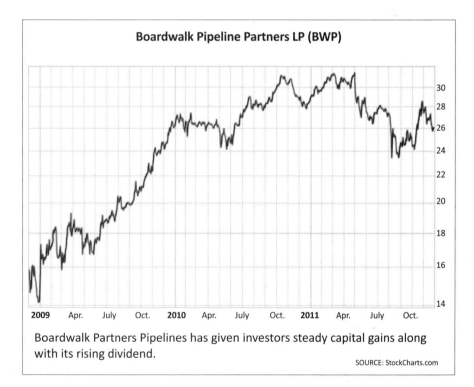

Boardwalk Pipeline Partners LP (BWP)

Boardwalk Partners Pipelines has given investors steady capital gains along with its rising dividend.

SOURCE: StockCharts.com

That's because 60 percent of this MLP is owned by Loews Corporation (L), the value-oriented conglomerate run by the Tisch family. Its track record over the long term has been stellar, and it's applying that methodology to Boardwalk as well.

Boardwalk has recently completed several compression projects designed to increase capacity at its network. Its quarterly cash distribution has been raised to $0.5225 per unit, for an annual yield of approximately 8.2 percent.

With a record for increasing distributions, it's no surprise that since inception in 2005, this MLP has managed a 17 percent average annual return. That's amazing performance for a period that includes the 2007-2009 bear market!

In the past three years, however, Boardwalk has managed to break through to new highs even as the market collapsed. Armed with long-term, value-oriented management, this trend will likely continue.

CHAPTER 9

The Preferred Way to Invest for High Income and Low Risk

Investors looking for more stability and higher income without losing out on potential capital gains might want to take a closer look at the smaller world of preferred stocks.

What's preferred stock? It combines some of the upside potential of a stock with the stable, high-yielding payments of a bond. Preferred shareholders are higher up on the food chain than holders of common stock, so they're more likely to get a return of capital in the event of bankruptcy.

And, of course, they're first in line for dividend payments.

In fact, preferred shares issued by major banks still made payments during the credit crunch, even after dividends on the big banks' common stock got eliminated or slashed to a penny.

Now, most investors likely know about preferred stocks. But, the majority of investors likely haven't heard of a subset of preferred stocks called "trust preferreds."

They are typically issued at $25 per share. This lower price makes it easier for the average investor to pick up round lots (100 shares of stock) without putting too much capital to work in this sector.

Under this structure, the bank creates a trust, which in turn issues preferred shares. The sale of the shares is used to buy debt from the bank. Due to this structure, dividends from trust preferreds aren't eligible for the 15 percent dividend tax rate. That makes these shares ideal for investors in low-tax brackets (such as current retirees), or for retirement accounts like 401(k)s IRAs, and especially Roth IRAs.

The biggest concern with owning preferred stock is liquidity. While hundreds of millions of shares may trade daily on the major banks, preferred shares may see only a few hundred or thousand traded. Nevertheless, trust preferreds tend to offer yields in the 5 to 7 percent range.

Many bank stocks issue debt using the trust preferred model. For investors who want stable dividend payments without the possibility of a dividend cut, preferred trusts offer the ideal solution. With the low liquidity and relatively little information out there regarding preferreds, it's best to use a limit order when establishing a position so as not to overextend yourself.

Trust Preferred Payout #1:

Diverse Exposure to Preferreds: Nuveen Quality Preferred Income Fund (JTP)

For individual investors who want to avoid the risk of being in one or two thinly traded preferred shares, there's the Nuveen Quality Preferred Income Fund (JTP).

This fund invests 80 percent of its assets in preferred shares, and 20 percent in convertible debt. That gives investors an easy way to avoid the problem of selection in the small world of preferreds and convertibles.

The fund is primarily diversified into preferreds from insurance companies, banks, and media firms, reflective of the overall composition of the preferred market. So investors who are looking for returns outside the financial and media sectors might want to look elsewhere.

With a monthly payout of $0.05 per share, investors get an effective yield of 8.0 percent with some substantial diversification. It's certainly a better return than a bond, but preferred shareholders are lower down than pure bondholders if an underlying company goes bankrupt.

Based on the net asset value of the fund, shares are currently at an 8 percent discount to the total value of all the securities in the account. In other words, it's on sale.

Since this fund invests in both preferred debt and preferred stock, its income and distribution payouts are determined by interest rates. Since rates have been cut in the past few years, so has the distribution. That means that if interest rates rise, so would interest rates on new corporate debt, leading to higher payouts in the future.

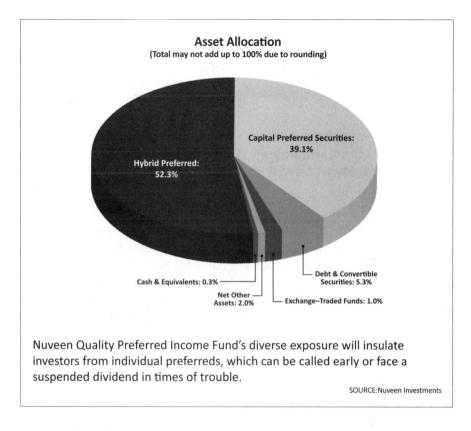

Asset Allocation
(Total may not add up to 100% due to rounding)

Capital Preferred Securities: 39.1%

Hybrid Preferred: 52.3%

Cash & Equivalents: 0.3%

Net Other Assets: 2.0%

Debt & Convertible Securities: 5.3%

Exchange–Traded Funds: 1.0%

Nuveen Quality Preferred Income Fund's diverse exposure will insulate investors from individual preferreds, which can be called early or face a suspended dividend in times of trouble.

SOURCE:Nuveen Investments

Trust Preferred Payout #2:

This Preferred Paid Out During the Credit Crunch: Bank of America Preferred Trust Series U

Individual bank preferreds trading at a discount to par could represent the best income opportunity of the next seven years. That's because bank-issued preferreds are considered part of a bank's Tier 1 capital, set to be phased out under the new legislation from the Dodd-Frank Wall Street Reform and Consumer Protection Act.

According to a RBC report on preferreds, this could be a boon to preferred holders: "The Tier 1 treatment will begin to be phased out in 2013, and will be phased out by the end of 2018. As a result, banks could call their hybrid and Trust Preferreds at some point during that time frame."

Within this space, one opportunity to pick up a bank preferred below par is the Bank of America Preferred Trust Series U. It trades at a 20.1 percent discount to its par value, meaning that if the bank called in the shares, investors would immediately realize a $5.17 gain.

That's in addition to the fat 7.41 percent yield, well in excess of Bank of America's penny-per-quarter dividend on its common shares. Depending on your brokerage, the ticker for this specific issue can vary, but it's usually BAC-U or BAC-PU.

Trust Preferred Payout #3:

One Foreign Bank Paying Off Its Bailout Funds: ING Perpetual Hybrid Trust Preferred

Investors seeking a slightly higher yield could look at the ING Perpetual Hybrid Trust Preferreds. This issuance has an effective yield of 9.53 percent, and trades at a 33 percent discount to par.

ING has a large U.S. exposure, despite being headquartered in the Netherlands. That leaves the bank better positioned than other counterparts in Europe amidst the throes of a credit crisis thanks to Greek and Italian debts. The bank's profitability allowed it to pay the final €3 billion in bailout money that it owed to its home country in 2011.

ING is now free to pay higher dividends on its common shares, or redeem its preferreds at par value.

The ticker for this preferred is ISF.

CHAPTER 10

These Funds Have You Covered For Alternative Sources of Income

The exchange-traded fund (ETF) universe has exploded over fourfold since 2003, and new funds continue to emerge on the market, focusing on everything from agricultural commodities to country-specific opportunities divided by industry and market capitalization.

For investors still stuck in the 1990s, an exchange-traded fund is typically a basket of assets, such as stocks, bonds, or commodities. It trades on a stock exchange, like a stock, and typically trades close to the net asset value of all the things it owns. Some ETFs track an index, and some track specific sectors or trends.

Compared to mutual funds, ETFs offer substantial advantages.

ETFs have low trading costs, tax efficiency, and lower management fees than mutual funds, making them the next evolutionary step in markets for individual investors with a need to diversify their portfolios against a variety of risks.

Since most ETFs either track a specific market or specific subsets of a market (such as a Chinese small-cap ETF), the focus is typically on the potential capital gains.

While many exchange-traded funds offer little to investors looking for current income, there are some notable exceptions. ETFs focused on dividend-producing companies, for example, will sometimes pass through some of that income to shareholders.

ETFs making specific investments in the MLP and REIT sector, for example, have no qualms about offering investors the opportunity to enjoy the advantages of this sector without the risk of a specific company going bankrupt.

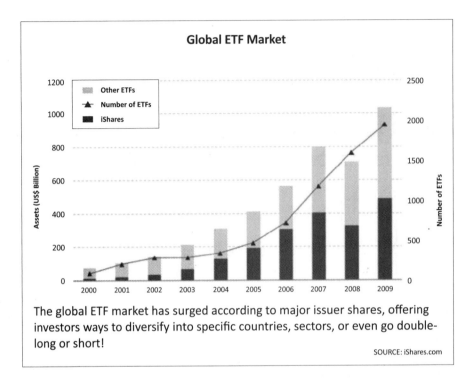

Global ETF Market

The global ETF market has surged according to major issuer shares, offering investors ways to diversify into specific countries, sectors, or even go double-long or short!

SOURCE: iShares.com

But, other funds are in another league when it comes to paying shareholders now for the risk of owning their shares: covered-call funds.

Covered-call funds seek to generate fat income off the volatility of a portfolio of stocks. This strategy employs the sales of call options against a position of stock to generate income.

Ideally, the call will expire worthless and the holder will keep the money from the sale. If the stock rises and hits the strike price of the call sold, the investor keeps the premium, but has to hand over the stock.

That's not necessarily a bad thing. By using this strategy, investors can set the price they get for the stock. By setting a sale price for the shares in advance, an investor can take some of the emotion out of letting go of a position.

Most investors who normally wouldn't touch an option have no problem selling calls against a position they own. Even conservative investors will use this strategy to boost the income of blue-chip stocks like IBM, or even to generate a yield off companies that don't pay a dividend like Berkshire Hathaway.

How do covered calls work? They're actually one of the most simple and low-risk option trades out there.

Let's say you bought shares of a company at $25 a while back and shares have doubled to $50. You expect further gains, but think the stock will trade in a narrow range for a few months. Meanwhile, your neighbor Bob is looking to buy this stock six months from now. So, you sell him a call option six months out on your stock for $6.

You will make an instant $6 from the sale. You get to keep that money. You also still own the stock.

Remember, Bob only has the *option* to buy the stock from you, so you keep collecting the dividend, too.

And, as long as the stock doesn't go above $56 in the next six months, you make a nice sum of money.

Say you know this stock well (in my example, of course!). You know it is a solid company that pays a nice dividend (4 percent) and that it will likely go up in the *long term*.

In the *short term*, however, you are equally confident the market will remain flat, and that it might even drop, perhaps substantially. By selling this call option, you make nice income now and you protect yourself.

The odds are in your favor. More than likely the stock will not go up to $56, so Bob will not cash in on his *option* to buy the stock from you. You get the income and you get to keep your stock.

You protect yourself in this way: If the stock market does drop substantially in value and shares of the company you own goes down with it, you at least collected the $6 premium from Bob.

And you still have your long-term stock to hold. With a cost basis of $25, the $6 premium you received from selling the call is a fat 24 percent return on your original cost! If you can get substantial premiums often enough without having the stock "called away," you'll generate substantial gains above and beyond dividends.

With covered-call funds, managers look for companies with the best option premiums available to generate the best short-term income. It's the kind of strategy most investors can employ on one or two stocks they own at a time, given that individual stock's volatility, but these funds allow investors to take advantage of this on a bigger scale.

Most of these funds offer yields in the 8 to 10 percent range. For investors who don't need current income, this high yield allows for faster wealth compounding in a diversified portfolio of blue-chip stocks. Some even pay monthly!

One caveat: At the time of writing this report, markets aren't seeing a lot of volatility. In fact, the so-called "fear gauge" of the market, the Volatility Index, is at lows last seen in 2007 before markets blew up. Fear breeds bigger premiums in options. If markets start seeing some bigger moves or have another major decline, volatility could pick up and these funds could see their performance improve, even if stocks get knocked around in the process.

Covered-Call Opportunity #1:

International Diversification: ING Global Equity Dividend & Premium Opportunity Portfolio Fund

One solid play in the covered-call fund universe is ING's Global Equity Dividend & Premium Opportunity Portfolio Fund (IGD).

That's because this fund invests only about one-third of its 65-to-90-stock portfolio in American companies. The other companies

The Breakdown of ING's Global Equity Dividend & Premium Opportunity Portfolio Fund's (IGD) Holdings	
Top Holdings % of Total Investments as of 10/31/2011	
E. ON AG	2.08%
Zurich Financial Services AG	1.93%
ENI S.p.A.	1.88%
Total SA	1.81%
Vinci SA	1.73%
Sanofi	1.71%
Royal Dutch Shell PLC	1.71%
General Electric Co.	1.69%
Merck & Co., Inc.	1.64%
Abbott Laboratories	1.62%
Total	17.8%

SOURCE: ING Group

are mostly spread in Europe, Japan, Australia, and South Korea.

There's also substantial industry diversification. The largest sector, finance, represents only about 20 percent of the entire portfolio.

More importantly, with the fund's strategy of writing covered calls, the fund can pay out a $0.10 *monthly* dividend. That's a mouth-watering **13.1 percent** at the fund's current price in the $9.00 range.

Investors would be wise to consider this fund for income rather than capital appreciation. The fund has hundreds of positions, so the best reason to own this fund is for the covered calls the company writes to generate income.

Covered-Call Opportunity #2:

Large-Cap American Value: Madison/Claymore Covered Call & Equity Strategy Fund

A quarterly dividend player with an **9.9 percent** yield, the Madison/Claymore Fund (MCN) focuses on generating income from large-cap American companies, with a focus on technology, healthcare, financial, and consumer companies.

MCN trades at a 11.5 percent discount to its NAV, offering investors a slight discount to the underlying stocks it owns in its portfolio, with the added allure of a high yield secured by covered call writing.

Madison/Claymore Fund's Top 10 Holdings as of 10/31/2011	
Google Inc	4.15%
Target	3.99%
Visa Inc	3.92%
Microsoft	3.50%
Gilead Sciences Inc	3.43%
State Street Corp	3.17%
Cisco Systems	3.11%
Wells Fargo	3.05%
Best Buy	2.94%
Hewlett-Packard	2.68%

SOURCE: Guggenheim Funds

Covered-Call Opportunity #3:

Dividend Growth Meets Covered-Call Writing: Blackrock Enhanced Dividend Achievers Trust

In 2005, Blackrock started its Enhanced Dividend Achievers Trust (BDJ) with dividends in mind. The company noted that, "since 1926, more than 40 percent of the 10.4 percent return of the S&P 500 Index has consisted of dividends and dividend reinvestment."

That's why its top holdings are well-recognized big-cap names such as IBM, Chevron, Caterpillar, ExxonMobil, and Johnson & Johnson.

Like most covered-call ETFs, the focus is on current income, and not on share price appreciation. However, in the past two years, shares have advanced substantially in addition to providing substantial income.

However, by combining the power of a dividend-growth portfolio with a covered-call strategy, the fund can pay out a fat dividend of 9.8 percent per year.

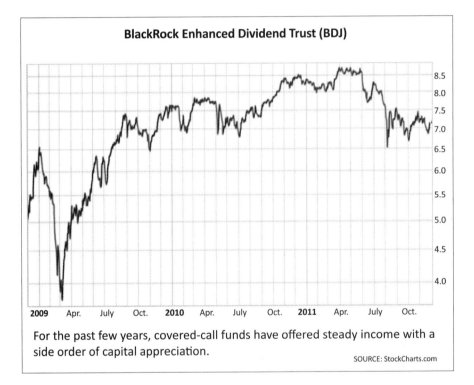

BlackRock Enhanced Dividend Trust (BDJ)

For the past few years, covered-call funds have offered steady income with a side order of capital appreciation.

SOURCE: StockCharts.com

Publicly Traded Private Equity Offering Fat Yields: Business Development Companies

Let's face facts: The wealthy are different from most investors. They can invest in private placements — and own part of a company before it goes public. They can invest in startups without being a partner or putting in the work of an owner. Either way, they can get fatter returns than bonds or common stocks for doing so.

But, that doesn't mean average investors are out of luck. One corporate structure that's publicly traded offers exposure to small, fast-growth companies that need access to capital. They're called business development companies (BDCs), and they offer investors substantial current income for the risk of investing in a pool of small businesses.

Structured like a REIT, a BDC builds and manages a portfolio of investments in small businesses. Some take an ownership stake, and some instead take warrants and debt so the company's ownership isn't diluted. Eventually the company stake is sold off, the company IPOs, or the debt is fully repaid.

Either way, these companies make regular payments to the BDC. Then the BDC turns around and pays out 90 percent to shareholders. That means investors get in on small, fast-growing companies, but also get fat cash payouts every 90 days.

In today's lending environment, where most banks simply don't want to make loans, BDCs are filling in the gap, and profiting handsomely from doing so. BDCs today are paying out dividends to shareholders in the 7 to 10 percent range.

Some of the biggest BDCs overleveraged and got burned during the credit crisis. That's why it's important to select a BDC with a clean balance sheet and a diversified number of investments.

BDC Opportunity #1:

Funding Tomorrow's New Technologies Today: Hercules Technologies Growth Capital

Hercules Technologies Growth Capital (HTGC) offers exposure to a wide variety of small technology companies, including medical devices, clean technology, communications equipment, and even biotech. It currently has investments with over 80 companies. That's a diverse subset of industries, each sending HTGC checks on a regular basis.

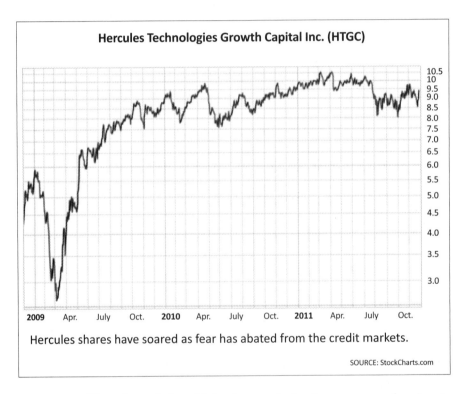

Hercules Technologies Growth Capital Inc. (HTGC)

Hercules shares have soared as fear has abated from the credit markets.

SOURCE: StockCharts.com

Unlike other BDCs which take a stake in the company they invest in, Hercules traditionally lends to these growing companies. This means Hercules won't see fat gains if it sells its stake later or if the company goes public.

What it does mean for the company that goes public, however, is a higher retained stake. In other words, the value of the company doesn't get as diluted along the way — a boon to any future prospective buyer.

Hercules' 9.7 percent yield is more than supported by earnings.

Combined with capital appreciation, HTGC has trounced the returns of the overall market.

The company trades at a discount book value and has a substantial cash stake of $75 million, about the same as the company's annual revenue. There's some debt on the books as well, but the BDC is still

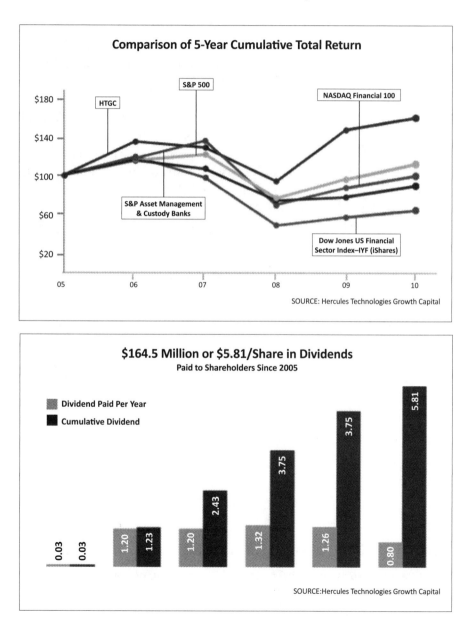

underleveraged relative to peers. The forward PE ratio of the company is 8, substantially less than the broad stock market as a whole.

Shares have fully recovered from the lows of the credit crisis, reflecting the strength of the company's underlying portfolio.

BDC Opportunity #2:

Ares Capital Corporation to the Rescue!

With a focus on restructuring, recapitalization, and rescue financing, Ares Capital (ARCC) has carved out a unique niche among BDCs, which usually focus on providing funding to companies at an earlier stage of growth.

Nevertheless, this method has led to a well-diversified portfolio of companies across a substantial number of industries.

But Ares isn't just rescuing small companies that have fallen on hard times. Ares absorbed one of its main competitors, the overleveraged Allied Capital, in 2010. This move has substantially increased its position in the BDC universe.

Profits remain fat — the company's most recent profit margin was

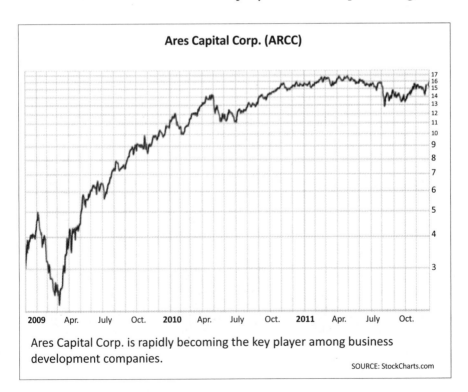

Ares Capital Corp. (ARCC)

2009   Apr.   July   Oct.   **2010**   Apr.   July   Oct.   **2011**   Apr.   July   Oct.

Ares Capital Corp. is rapidly becoming the key player among business development companies.

SOURCE: StockCharts.com

Ares Capital	
Industry	**Percentage**
Investment Funds	21%
Healthcare Services	16%
Business Services	12%
Restaurants & Food Services	9%
Consumer Products	8%
Financial Services	7%
Education	5%
Manufacturing	4%
Other Services	3%
Telecommunications	2%
Food & Beverage	2%
Retail	2%
Commercial Real Estate	1%
Wholesale Distribution	4%
Other	4%

SOURCE:www.AresCapitalCorp.com

a staggering 138.47 percent! Revenue growth is up more than double year over year, which is why it can pay out a sizable dividend of 9.92 percent.

Shares trade close to book value of the company's assets, and the firm has a respectable forward PE ratio of 8.2.

BDC Opportunity #3:

A Value-Oriented BDC: Apollo Investment Corp.

With a focus on significant free cash flow, experienced management, and a strong competitive industry, Apollo Investment Corp. (AINV) is the BDC equivalent of the large acquisitions made by Berkshire Hathaway.

The company's investments are all over the map, from consulting

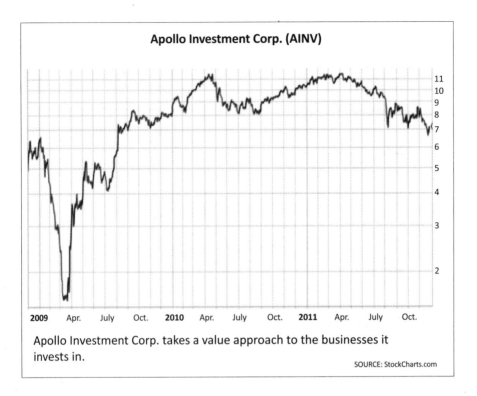

Apollo Investment Corp. (AINV)

Apollo Investment Corp. takes a value approach to the businesses it invests in.

SOURCE: StockCharts.com

firms to tire distribution centers to education companies to hotels. With investments in over 65 companies, Apollo invests in both debt and equity stakes.

In the past year, shares have range-traded between $6 and $12 ... while paying out a 16.8 percent dividend following the market selloff in the fall of 2011.

Apollo is attracting the interest of at least one major investor: Billionaire George Soros added 10,900 shares in the first quarter of 2011. Whether he's investing for the company's fat yield or portfolio of diverse, small companies is still up for debate.

CHAPTER 12

Income Outside the U.S. Dollar: Currency Plays Offering Higher Interest Rates

U ltra-low interest rates aren't strictly an American phenomenon. Europe is in the throes of a series of country-specific debt crises. Japan is entering its third "lost decade" as a result of a burst bubble and now a series of disasters.

But other regions are faring well. In fact, some are outright *thriving* to the point where their central bankers are concerned. This means that they've been hiking interest rates to cool growth . . . and that their currencies offer investors a substantially higher interest rate than the dollar.

For American investors, that's a good thing. Investors can globally diversify without chasing the latest stock bubble in China and other emerging markets. How? By purchasing these high-interest currencies with their no-yield dollars. In other words, foreign exchange, or forex.

While forex might bring to mind thoughts of currency traders over-leveraging and trying to turn a one-pip move ($0.0001) into a hefty gain, there are several ways to safely invest in currencies without leverage *and* generate income doing so.

These methods include foreign bonds, which typically have higher yields than U.S. bonds, unleveraged currency funds, which pay monthly interest, and currency CDs from a leading American bank that offer downside protection against unpredictable currency moves.

Currency Opportunity #1:
Grab Higher Interest Rates With a Top Foreign Bond Fund
With a roughly 6.2 percent yield and a monthly dividend schedule, it's clear to see why the Aberdeen Asia-Pacific Income Fund (FAX) is one

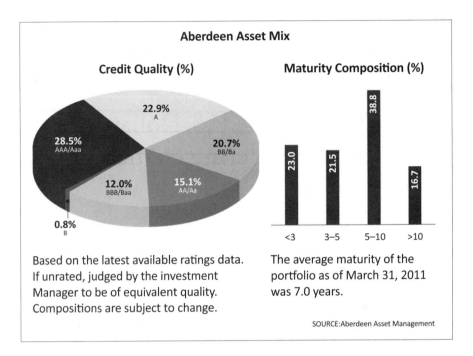

Aberdeen Asset Mix

Credit Quality (%)

22.9%
A

28.5%
AAA/Aaa

20.7%
BB/Ba

12.0%
BBB/Baa

15.1%
AA/Aa

0.8%
B

Based on the latest available ratings data. If unrated, judged by the investment Manager to be of equivalent quality. Compositions are subject to change.

Maturity Composition (%)

23.0   21.5   38.8   16.7

<3   3–5   5–10   >10

The average maturity of the portfolio as of March 31, 2011 was 7.0 years.

SOURCE:Aberdeen Asset Management

bond fund suited for low-risk, income-oriented investors.

The fund is 52.5 percent invested in Asian bonds. While 35.2 percent of the fund is in U.S. dollar-backed bonds, those bonds are issued by Asian companies. The largest single country exposure is in Australia, followed by South Korea and Hong Kong.

Over 70 percent of the bonds have an A-credit rating or higher, and the average maturity of the bond portfolio is seven years. As for its allocation, 46.4 percent of the fund's portfolio is in corporate bonds, followed by 49 percent in government debt.

Currency Opportunity #2:

Monthly Interest Payments From Unleveraged Foreign Currencies

The dollar's decline has been well documented in other parts of this report. Investors seeking a place to protect the value of their money while still staying in "cash" may want to consider currency funds.

These funds trade with the liquidity of stocks, and most offer monthly payouts representative of the interest earned. Best of all, since some currencies tend to trade in the opposite direction of the U.S. dollar, these funds offer a convenient way to diversify into an appreciating asset. Of course, that means if fear strikes markets and investors rush to the dollar, like they did in late 2008, these currencies could sharply correct.

Here are three currency funds that pay monthly interest payments, and are in currencies set to rise as the dollar falls.

1) CURRENCY SHARES AUSTRALIAN DOLLAR TRUST (FXA) Australia was barely touched by the recent recession. This commodity-rich country has been moving full steam ahead developing its natural resources to sell to its Asian neighbors — particularly China.

Despite a few rate hikes from Australia's central bank, the Australian dollar has continued to appreciate. In fact, the currency now trades at an all-time high, and at a premium to the U.S. dollar.

In the past 12 months, FXA has paid out over $3.585 in monthly interest payments, for a current yield of approximately 3.8 percent.

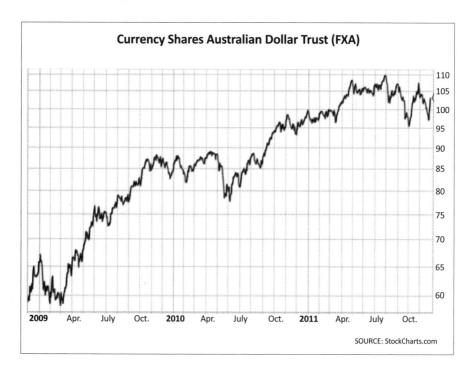

2) CURRENCY SHARES SWEDISH KRONA TRUST (FSX) While Sweden may seem an unlikely place for investors to park cash, the Swedish

Currency Shares Swedish Krona Trust (FXS)

Although it's not the first place on someone's radar for a strong currency, the Swedish krona has been appreciating steadily against the U.S. dollar.

SOURCE: StockCharts.com

krona has held up well, especially compared to its no-yield neighbors in the euro.

The yield on the krona isn't as high as on currencies such as the Australian dollar. However, the Swedish krona also has failed to break through its old highs against the dollar. Bottom line: The Swedish krona has upside potential in addition to the income generated from interest.

Sweden's central bank hasn't been as aggressive about raising rates as other banks, and most central bank watchers anticipate anywhere from one to three more interest rate hikes from Sweden's central bank in 2011.

Monthly payments have only begun since the start of 2011, but based on current payments, the fund is set to pay out in the 1.0 to 1.5 percent range.

3) CURRENCY SHARES MEXICAN PESO TRUST (FXM) Investors can grab monthly payments in more exotic currencies like the Mexican peso with the CurrencyShares Mexican Peso Trust (FXM). The Mexican peso is the currency trader's play of choice to profit from rising oil prices, although this currency is more prone to fluctuate than the other ones mentioned in this report.

Based on trailing payments, this fund offers a 2.4 percent yield.

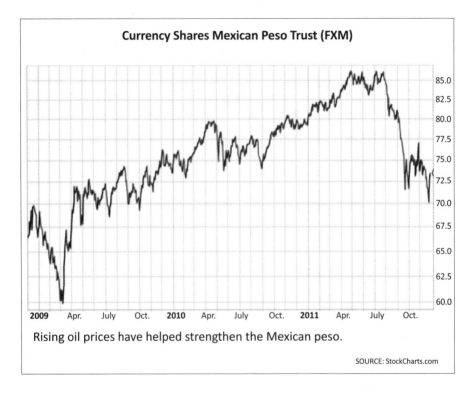

Currency Shares Mexican Peso Trust (FXM)

Rising oil prices have helped strengthen the Mexican peso.

SOURCE: StockCharts.com

Currency Opportunity #3:

One American Bank Offers Forex CDs With FDIC Insurance

There's one way to invest in higher-yielding foreign currency with ZERO risk of downside losses. All you need to do is to call one American bank and invest in one of their certificates of deposit.

The bank is called EverBank, and it offers everything from single-currency CDs with short maturities, to longer-dated CDs with multi-currency exposure. A few even seek to capitalize on the gains from precious metals!

These products are FDIC-insured. So, worst-case scenario, even if every currency in one of the bank's portfolios goes bust, investors can still recover their original capital. Of course, from what we've seen with the dollar's performance, that's a bit unlikely.

A word of caution: Investing in a CD carries substantial liquidity risks compared to the other investments in this report, so this investment isn't ideal for funds that you may need converted to cash at a moment's notice.

Also, minimums on EverBank products typically start at $10,000, so its products are best for those with a large pool of capital looking to preserve their capital rather than aggressively grow it.

For more information on currency-specific CDs and currency basket CDs, visit https://www.everbank.com/personal/foreign-currencies.aspx. You can also call at (888) 882-3837 anytime to open a new bank account.

How to Get Your Retirement
Income Portfolio on Track With
a Three-Step Plan to Generate
Substantial Income in Your
Retirement Years

CHAPTER 13

Step #1: Set Up an Income Plan That's Right for You

While we've covered some of the more unique opportunities out there for income needs, we couldn't write this report with your individual financial situation in mind. You'll want to take the time to review some of these opportunities with the other financial decision makers in your household, as well as a financial adviser and accountant.

In order to set up an income plan that's right for you, you'll need to take into account your current and future goals, and how income-oriented investments can help you achieve them.

But don't forget: There are risks involved with all investments. Income investments could be adversely affected by the performance of the underlying business, changes in the interest rate, or liquidity fears, among numerous other factors (including unforeseeable ones).

That said, we've put together three model income plans.

The first is designed for a lower-risk, lower return for ultra-conservative investors, expected to generate some income and a 5 percent annual return. For conservative investors, we have a model that shoots for 10 percent returns with a mix of income and capital gains. For moderate investors, we go further up the yield and risk curve to show a model portfolio that can produce returns of 15 percent per year.

Remember: These model portfolios are subjective and are concentrated in only a few positions. As such, they may lack diversification and tax efficiency specific to your individual investment needs. We encourage you to consult your financial planner and accountant for the implications of any investment.

Ultra-Conservative Investor: Achieving 5% Returns

For the ultra-conservative investor, preservation of capital is more important than shooting for the biggest yield or potential for capital gains. Fortunately, we've covered investments in this report that offer investors their original capital back. Combined with some higher-yielding investments, the portfolio can offer a 5 percent annual return. There's a catch, of course: The prospect for substantial capital gains is limited.

The first must-own category for the ultra-conservative investor is trust preferred shares — so long as the investor buys them below par. Since these shares have to eventually be redeemed at par, there's little risk of capital loss if the position is held until shares are called.

The next low-risk investment can be found in the FDIC-insured products from EverBank. Again, by holding one of their CDs until maturity, investors can lock in gains on currency moves and still protect their original investment capital.

There's a bit more risk involved, but with the high yield on a covered-call ETF, investors can book a substantial income from a portfolio of stocks with lower volatility than overall stock indices.

Although more volatile, the tax benefits of owning a pass-through entity like a REIT or MLP may offset the extra risk for an ultra-conservative investor.

Sample Ultra-Conservative Portfolio:

- 30% Bank of America Preferred Series U (BAC-U)
- 30% EverBank All-Weather Portfolio
- 20% ING Global Equity Dividend (IGD)
- 20% Kinder Morgan Partners (KMP)

Approximate Weighted Yield: 6.69%; 60% of portfolio is capital protected (if BAC-U is bought below par value of $25), with some upside potential on KMP and IGD.

Conservative Investor: Achieving 10% returns

For a conservative investor looking for a 10 percent minimum total return per year, more options are available. One holding could include a REIT, which offers a sizable yield and capital appreciation.

Another sector worth owning for the conservative investor would be an MLP, with perhaps a higher exposure to this sector than the ultra-conservative investor.

Finally, conservative investors might want to look at currency funds. They'll pay out modest monthly dividends, and provide gains against the dollar's long-term decline. Of course, there's no FDIC protection, and a major market correction and subsequent fear could cause a dollar rally in the short term.

Sample Conservative Portfolio:

- 25% Realty Income (O)
- 25% Boardwalk Pipeline Partners (BWP)
- 15% CurrencyShares Australian Dollar Trust (FXA)
- 35% Nuveen Quality Preferred Income Fund (JPZ)

Approximate Weighted Yield: 7.2%; portfolio has moderate upside potential on FXA and JPZ, BWP and O, making total returns of 10% very achievable.

Moderate Investor: Achieving 15% returns

The moderate investor, looking to make 15 percent returns each year, has to go into some of the riskier income assets mentioned in this report. For example, just by buying shares of mortgage REIT Annaly Capital Management, an investor could see a dividend near 15 percent per year — but shares could sell off big if interest rates rise.

Investments for this investor include business development companies, covered-call ETFs, MLPs, REITs, and a portfolio of dividend growth stocks to achieve these kinds of returns.

Investments based on cash, bonds, or preferreds will typically generate insufficient returns in this overall portfolio to be of any benefit.

Sample Moderate Portfolio:

- 20% ING Global Equity Dividend & Premium Opportunity Fund (IGD)
- 30% Apollo Capital Group (AINV)
- 5% each in dividend growth stocks Kraft, J&J, and Cisco (KFT, JNJ, CSCO)
- 15% Buckeye Partners MLP (BPL)
- 20% Annaly Capital Management Mortgage REIT (NLY)

Approximate Weighted Yield 9.3%; substantial potential for capital gains on AINV, KFT, JNJ, CSCO, with moderate potential upside in IGD, BPL, and NLY to potentially bring total returns to 15% per year.

CHAPTER 14

Step #2: How You Can Turn $50,000 Into $1 Million

With an income plan in place, it will be substantially easier to make the necessary calculations to determine the future value of your investment portfolio. That's because income-producing investments tend to have lower volatility, which means the returns are much steadier.

Using a variety of online sites, you can plug in your current account value, the expected return from your portfolio, and any other additions you plan to make along the way to find out what the future of your portfolio will look like.

By using your current yield as your expected return and ignoring potential capital gains, you can create a very conservative metric that represents a "worst-case" scenario for your long-term portfolio. But let's be realistic and assume at least some capital appreciation occurs as well.

Let's say you start today with $50,000 in your retirement portfolio. Using some of the income investments in this report, let's assume that returns from both income and capital gains end up at around 10 percent. What does that $50,000 turn into in 20 years?

Using the compound interest calculator from the website MyAmortizationChart.com, we get the following chart:

Effects of Compound Interest

Year	Starting Balance	Earned Interest	Ending Balance
1	$50,000.00	$5,235.65	$55,235.65
2	$55,235.65	$5,783.89	$61,019.54
3	$61,019.55	$6,389.54	$67,409.09
4	$67,409.09	$7,058.61	$74,467.70
5	$74,467.70	$7,797.74	$82,265.45
6	$82,265.45	$8,614.27	$90,879.71
7	$90,879.71	$9,516.29	$100,396.01
8	$100,396.01	$10,512.77	$110,908.78
9	$110,908.78	$11,613.60	$122,522.38
10	$122,522.38	$12,829.69	$135,352.07
11	$135,352.07	$14,173.13	$149,525.21
12	$149,525.21	$15,657.24	$165,182.45
13	$165,182.45	$17,296.76	$182,479.21
14	$182,479.21	$19,107.96	$201,587.17
15	$201,587.17	$21,108.81	$222,695.98
16	$222,695.98	$23,319.18	$246,015.16
17	$246,015.16	$25,761.00	$271,776.16
18	$271,776.16	$28,458.52	$300,234.67
19	$300,234.67	$31,438.49	$331,673.17
20	$331,673.17	$34,730.51	$366,403.68
Totals		$316,403.68	$366,403.68

SOURCE: MyAmortizationChart.com

Over $350,000! But take a look at that middle category: earned interest. By the 20th year, thanks to the power of compounding, your income from this portfolio is 70 percent of your original investment!

That's just assuming you didn't add in any additional capital to fund your retirement.

If you can compound your wealth faster, the gains become even more magnified. At a 15 percent return over the same 20-year time period, the same $50,000 becomes over $983,000.

Kick in another $10 a month over that time period, and you can clear the $1,000,000 mark.

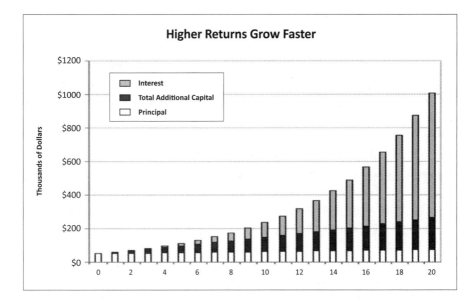

The Path to Prosperity: Steady Returns Over Long Periods

Investors looking at the power of compound returns can take away four simple lessons:

- **First, you need quality investments.** This year's "hot sector" may be next year's laggard. A company with a great story might not be able to perform as well financially as its CEO performs during CNBC interviews. Since the real power of compounding wealth comes from reinvesting, you'll need to *be in assets that can continue to grow and perform well over the long term.*

- **The second lesson here is often cited as the first rule of investing:** *Don't lose money!* A 50 percent loss needs to double just to get back to even. A 90 percent loss needs a 900 percent gain to break even! It doesn't matter how well your winners perform if you hang on to losers that keep declining. That's why quality is so important. *Low quality investments carry the risk of permanent loss of capital.* For speculative positions, use trailing stop losses so that you can lock in big gains without seeing them turn into substantial losses.

- **Third, you can get an extra "kicker" to your returns in the early years by adding additional capital, even small amounts.**

Since compound interest takes time to work its magic, investors who can't start with a lump sum can still enjoy the benefits of compound interest by adding capital regularly. For example: Over a 15-year period, an investor can increase total return by $83,584 by simply putting away $200 a month in an account earning 10 percent interest.

- **Finally, and possibly most importantly,** *time is your friend.* Patience is the name of the game. Like the tale of the tortoise and the hare, the secret to getting rich isn't a dash after the best-returning assets. Rather, it's about the slow accumulation of wealth. The biggest gains from compound inflation occur in later years.

It may be difficult to compound quickly if you're close to retirement and need current income. However, it sure is nice to receive a 10 percent return on your nest egg instead of a paltry 1 percent that a CD pays.

And, it's never too early to educate children and grandchildren with this concept, so you can best make use of their biggest asset: time.

Attempting to get rich quickly is usually just that — an attempt. In the world of investing, the real returns come from slow and steady gains, grown over long periods of time. You can't plant a seed on a Monday and expect a full-grown tree by the weekend!

CHAPTER 15

Step #3: Stay on Course to Power Your Retirement Income With Respected Guidance

Let's face reality: In this report, you've seen that most baby boomers are unprepared to retire. They simply don't have the savings. They'll have to delay or defer their retirement — possibly indefinitely.

On the investment front, most fixed-income investments offer paltry yields. Those already retired on a big portfolio of government bonds have had to cut back on their standard of living. The income just isn't there.

Baby boomers won't rely on bonds to build their wealth. They need higher income, and they need to build up their retirement funds over years, not decades.

Make no mistake: It's daunting. Social Security benefits will likely be cut and the retirement age is set to ratchet up over time.

With the power of higher-yielding investments and compound interest, however, all is not lost. The longer rates remain significantly low, the more likely it is that investors will continue to be drawn to higher yielding, but riskier investments.

The implication is clear: **High-income investments should continue to perform well in a zero-interest-rate world.**

Of course, you'll need to steer clear of some of the riskier investments in the high-income universe.

For instance, many REITs don't operate as conservatively as the ones outlined in this report. They could face cash-flow problems in the wake of another credit crunch.

Some MLPs have direct exposure to commodity prices, and another major price drop, like the 10 percent daily decline in oil on May 5, 2011, could instantly erase substantial gains. Fortunately, there are always opportunities. You don't have to shoot for the moon on the next "hot stock" being touted by some talking head.

Behind all the financial metrics and other data, staying the course involves something else: you. More specifically, your patience, and your willingness to stay the course, no matter what markets do. Keeping your emotions out of your investment decisions just might be the most important thing you can do as an investor.

That means when everyone else is scrambling for the exits, you can pick up quality investments on the cheap. When everyone is clamoring to buy some hot stock, you can sell it to them. Let the emotions of others set bargains . . . and be prepared to buy.

CHAPTER 16

Bonus Step: Stay Informed In a Continually Changing Investment World

L et's be honest: The companies mentioned here will see their performance vary. What may be a good investment at the time this report was written might not be by the time you're ready to build your safe retirement income portfolio.

That's why it's critical to stay informed of developments in the financial world. It's also why this report comes with access to three financial newsletters to help you stay knowledgeable and profitable no matter what happens next.

Combined, they form the perfect investment weapon.

These newsletters are: **Financial Intelligence Report, Gold Stock Adviser, and The Franklin Prosperity Report.**

Financial Intelligence Report

Unlike many other financial newsletters that have a narrow focus, **Financial Intelligence Report** is written for the all-around investor who wants to know about stocks, bonds, real estate, commodities, precious metals, and more. Our team scours the world to find the best investment opportunities and share them with our readers.

Over the past six years, we issued 215 investment recommendations to our **Financial Intelligence Report** members. Were all of them winners? No, of course not.

But out of those 215 investment recommendations . . . *181 of them were winning picks.*

Of those 181 winners, an astounding one-third (60) returned gains of 50 percent or more for our subscribers. And, nine recommendations blew through the 100 percent return mark and had *triple-digit gains.*

You may have had $10,000 invested in the S&P 500 in December 2003. Today, that's nearly $15,000. But, if you had invested the same $10,000 into the recommendations in the monthly issues of **Financial Intelligence Report**, you would have over $37,000 — more than twice as much!

Gold Stock Adviser

This is an elite gold stock advisory service unlike any other: We focus in like a laser on the handful of undervalued large-cap and mid-tier mining companies that could produce 50 percent ... 100 percent ... even 250 percent gains or more.

Is it too late to invest in gold stocks now? Not by a long shot! In fact, anyone who tells you the bull market in gold is over hasn't been paying attention.

People said the same thing about the stock market back in the late 1980s — when the Dow was at 2,500! After seven years of skyrocketing stock prices, these permabears claimed the market simply couldn't go any higher.

If you had listened to them then, you would have missed out on the Dow's climb to 14,000.

The truth is, most bull market cycles last **15 to 20 years!** Gold stocks actually bottomed in 1962 and moved higher until 1980 — an 18-year bull market in gold.

At the moment, however, we are only **a few years** into the current cycle.

Gold stocks bottomed out in the fourth quarter of 2000 and gold itself bottomed in April 2001. That's why I believe there should be at least another five to 10 years to go in this run-up.

The Franklin Prosperity Report

Fact: The vast majority of households with annual incomes of more than $100,000 have little accumulated wealth! Even America's high-earners are unprepared for a sound retirement.

The explanation for this apparent paradox is simple: Most of us have forgotten the virtues of saving and frugality that have made the United States the envy of the world.

To become wealthy and secure, most of us don't need to increase our income. Instead, we need to learn how to manage the money we have better.

That's why we're including a trial to **The Franklin Prosperity Report.**

The Franklin Prosperity Report's clear, simple language will teach you *dozens of practical steps you can take to manage your income better, cut your expenses, plan your finances, and live within your means.*

The payoff: Just by changing your habits, you can become truly wealthy and never have to worry about how you are going to pay your bills or what happens if you get laid off.

Take a look at these newsletters and decide for yourself if you would like to keep them. If you're serious about building the kind of investment portfolio that can guarantee you peace of mind in retirement, you'll want the fountain of information that these monthly newsletters provide.

CONCLUSION

Today's investment environment can be very difficult. Trying to find solid returns without the nasty risks associated can be extremely difficult.

The high-income investments mentioned in this report are often ignored simply because most people don't know about them. In fact, most "financial experts" don't know about them.

These investments are great, but they are also just a start.

Each and every day brings new challenges. That is why it is so important to pay attention to the free newsletters you will be receiving. Through these newsletters we aim to protect and grow your wealth, giving you an edge . . . an almost unfair advantage . . . that few investors have.

Together we can build your dream retirement!

Andrew Packer is a financial editor with Moneynews.com. He has written investment services on small-cap value investing and shorting, and contributed big-cap international value investments to a monthly publication.

Andrew has been an avid investor since childhood. Starting with bullion and collectible coins, he expanded into mutual funds and stocks as a teenager. He has since added options, real estate and bonds to his personal portfolio.

His investment approach is based on value, growth at a reasonable price, high-income plays and any other opportunities presented by the market. After earning a BA in economics, Andrew has honed his analytical skills while working at various companies, including real estate research and private equity.

This report was also written with guidance from the Moneynews Financial Braintrust, which includes members such as Robert Wiedemer, author of *Aftershock*, Christopher Ruddy, founder and CEO of Newsmax Media, and other financial experts.